Palewell Pres

Playing with the Pieces

Our mental state – how it can deform or be
disgraced, tested past all limits and yet endure

Nick Alldridge

To Phil

Happy 50th

Nick

Palewell Press

Printed and bound in the United Kingdom

Published by Palewell Press http://palewellpress.co.uk

First Edition

ISBN 978-0-9556770-3-8

Dedication

To poets who read more than they write and listen when it's not
their turn to speak.

Acknowledgements

A version of 'Night scratchings' previously appeared in Poetic Licence issue 30 under the title 'I am the paper.'

Thanks to Peter Evans at Poets Anonymous, Angela Brodie and Caroline Vero at Beyond Words and Peter and Katherine at South Bank Poetry and Camilla Reeve without all of whom this would not be the collection that it is.

Thanks to Steve Rushton for good advice and to Charley, Orlanda, Arrianne, Ted, Patricia, Muhammad, Jim, Jo, Anne, Debby, Peter, Katherine, Ruth, Frank, Steve, Alec, Mary, Bart and many others for their kind words and encouragement.

Introduction

When I came to write this introduction I wanted to talk about what connects these individual poems that took over a decade to write. Rather than do so in my own words I would like to quote Dan Pallotta from his TED talk 'The dream we haven't dared to dream' who sums it up in prose more eloquently than I can:

"Well, that's just the price of progress, we say. You can go to the Moon or you can have stability in your family life. And we can't conceive of dreaming in both dimensions at the same time. And we don't set the bar much higher than stability when it comes to our emotional life. Which is why our technology for talking to one another has gone vertical, our ability to listen and understand one another has gone nowhere. Our access to information is through the roof, our access to joy, grounded. But this idea, that our present and our future are mutually exclusive, that to fulfill our potential for doing we have to surrender our profound potential for being, that the number of transistors on a circuit can be doubled and doubled, but our capacity for compassion and humanity and serenity and love is somehow limited is a false and suffocating choice."

If my words on the following pages touch your life and resonate, if one catches in your throat as you read it aloud or another gives you some comfort to know that you are not alone in how you feel or look at the world then I am satisfied. I have been told my poetry is brave, I only wish it to be authentic.

Nick Alldridge

Contents

Taking Life Apart 9

Soul 10

Night scratchings – Sonnet #105 11

After the pub – Sonnet #13 12

The voicemail 13

The letter – Sonnet #72 14

Sleep Apnoea 16

Dyspraxia Sonnet – #1100 17

Catastrophe – Sonnet #12 18

Guilt and betrayal – Sonnet #922 19

Triptych 20

A coincidence of time and space – Sonnet #531 22

Near death experience 23

Pivotal 24

The killer next-door 26

Dysfunctional 2 28

Anxiety – Sonnet #222 29

Try to understand 30

Learning to swear   Learning to let go 31

Be brave 32

The state of not knowing 33

Between times 34

The Quest for Knowledge 35

    Mythmatics – Sonnet #153 36

    The loss of innocence – Sonnet #14 37

    Dream worlds – Sonnet #196a 38

    Science and faith – Sonnet #196b 39

    She – Sonnet #196c 40

    Lightning catcher – Sonnet #196d 41

    The tyrant's lair – Sonnet #196e 42

    Losing control – Sonnet #196f 43

    Ghosts and echoes in the air – Sonnet #196g 44

    Regaining control – Sonnet #196h 45

    Of – Sonnet #196i 46

    Beauty and grace – Sonnet #196j 47

    When you were comatose – Sonnet #196k 48

    A world away – Sonnet #196l 49

    Find your own way back – Sonnet #196m 50

    Fundamental truths – Sonnet #196n 51

    The myth of predetermination – Sonnet #3 52

A New Arrangement 53

    Just then 54

    Subtraction – Sonnet #501 55

    After a period of absence – Sonnet #155 56

    A game of chess – Sonnet #64 57

    Insight 58

Forgiveness – Sonnet #2..59

Happy getting over me day 60

Self discovering..61

Labels – Sonnet #1101...62

November memories...63

Imprints 1 – Sonnet #1051a 64

Imprints 2 – Sonnet #1051b 65

Imprints 3 – Sonnet #1051c..66

Imprints 4 – Sonnet #1051d 67

Imprints 5 – Sonnet #1051e 68

Revelations 69

The next moon landing – Sonnet #27...................................70

Time – Sonnet #59...71

Carpe diem – Sonnet #111 72

Seasoned 73

Leaving..74

Coda..75

And now...76

<u>Taking Life Apart</u>

In the darkest night
suffer change or lose yourself;
barren trees may bud.

Soul

Easy to misplace something so light
or fail to hear her song – so quiet.

Lost in darkness, shuttered in a time of need,
the sprouting tip is lost within the seed.

Disinclined to flourish when the ground is hard and dry
You may not see her in the crevice where she hides

so softly seek her gentle whispers in your ear,
personal, intrinsic so you have to strain to hear.

She exists in contemplation, brings joy to solitude,
together you're inseparable, no-one can intrude.

Search for her in the morning, by the evening she may glow
and when you die of course, she shines for everyone to know.

Night scratchings – Sonnet #105

I have a pen and I must write
the private whisper urges me –
get it down now, this time, this place.
In this small room, beside this single bed,
so careless to have no paper.
No-one here to share these thoughts,
they must echo along my arm,
tingle into my flesh
and scrape up next to my wrist.
Here now, in this time and place,
this quiet solitary limb must suffice.
There will be other times
but not this time again;
It makes its mark on me.

After the pub – Sonnet #13

for Ken

There were things that we could only say
in the early hours of the morning,
outside the gates of a school
that neither of us had ever attended,
on the way back to your place,
for coffee and more chat.
Whatever it was we spoke about
it kept us sane.
But there were interruptions:
My girlfriend – your girlfriend;
Your girlfriend – my wife;
My wife – your suicide;
. . .
Can we talk about that?

The voicemail

I heard an old voicemail today,
it caught me unawares.
Three months ago my mother called,
"Nothing urgent, please ring me back."
I did, three months ago.
I cannot now.

But the sorrow was tinged with joy
because I rang her back
        and spoke to her
                and did all that she asked of me.
And it was nice to hear that voice.

I don't know why I saved it.
A miracle that such a simple message
        could mean so much
                and touch so deep.
I left the message there,
too bitter-sweet to play again,
too important to delete.

The letter – Sonnet #72

Writing words that no one will read;
the nib scratches memories across the page
pushing ink into the void.
This is how we say goodbye,
again,
reaffirm commitments, long since rendered obsolete,
promising a better past to come,
stating what was never said.
Here we seek redemption,
place our guilt inside the ink
and move on,
slowly: one line at a time,
hesitant, reluctant, but knowing –
we do not go alone.

Dysfunctional 1 – Sonnet #322

There are four ways of falling out of a tree,
three of them are clever the other one is me.
The whole world is falling between us three,
mother, father, daughter – what will we be?
We don't get to choose the roles we take,
any more than the choices, the other two make.
Swimming in the river, lying by the lake,
offering condolences – *for pity's sake*.
and I don't know what the words mean,
and I don't know where you've been.
It remains to be seen,
if my conscience is clean.
You count the fingers and I'll count the toes
and where it ends, nobody knows.

Sleep Apnoea

Every year is precious, but the shadow years were lost.
Every seed we planted was withered by the frost,
dried on the parched winds, that rattled dry bones on the sand,
scorched by day, split by ice as night sucked memories from the land
and slowly stole a life.

Dyspraxia Sonnet – #1100

Just a little bit adrift in time and space;
never quite sure of your exact location
or direction and rate of travel.
Easy to understand Heisenberg,
when you live his theory every day,
keeping time more or less – well less;
can't seem to get the rhythm right,
from one day to the next.
Interesting where this leads,
this different slant on where we reside,
how fixed we are or aren't.
Drop your preconceptions
to think outside the box
that cannot contain you.

Catastrophe – Sonnet #12

All that angry lava
and the poison gas
and thick black ash,
it all had to come from within;

it must be hollow afterwards,
on the point of collapse:
After the burning tears
the emptiness inside.

Sometimes there is no eruption,
just quake
and the tidal wave
and the aftershocks

and sometimes the ground opens
and swallows a house.

Guilt and betrayal – Sonnet #922

I cannot return to the past and she
cannot leave it. Like ghosts we walk
through each other's walls.
I have barely energy for the present,
yet, every time we meet, she drags up the past,
full of betrayals I can barely remember
and which I know were more complicated,
although I no longer recall exactly how.
Things happen in a different order, in our
separate heads, with wholly different weights
and implications. I acknowledge the guilt,
merited or undeserved,
aware that I cannot argue my case
and that it matters more to her.

Triptych

Three scenes unfolding out of memory;
all in the dark and damp, at the tail end of the year.

On the left:
A tower block with grass around,
hemmed in by a low brick wall,
then pavement, road – a common place.

Central scene:
A row of terraced houses dimly lit.
Between each pair a black path leads
to steps down to the cellar.

Right hand:
Suburban railway station,
footbridge across the track
and a train on platform one.

Action: One
Two figures cut across the corner;
The taller leads, I follow: leap
but one foot catches and I'm arse over tit,
upside down, still airborne – Cut.

Action: Two
Cutting corners once again,
to catch up with the group in front

but where I've crossed I've missed the path
and I'm disappearing out of view,
straight down – Cut.

Action: Three
People hurry up and down,
I'm rushing for the train
and trying to read the destination;
I miss my step. I'm falling down.
My knee has kissed a step below
the one my ankle's twisting on – Cut.

The catalogue of injuries, not in order:
A small cut between two fingers,
a bruised tail-bone,
and nothing – nothing at all.

The handrail saves me. Hand wrapped round
forcing my weight up and barely breaking stride,
I make the train, puzzled by the drop of blood
from where I gripped the metal.

The other two: I'm saved by alcohol;
so relaxed I went with each fall,
flipped over the wall, lying winded on my back.
And the other time, six feet down,
each foot of mine landing on a different stair,
and me – just standing there.

A coincidence of time and space – Sonnet #531

An accident of fate, a coincidence of time and space, turns an event from what is known, perhaps read about in newspapers or presented to us on the radio or television news, into that which is experienced.

The sky was a brilliant blue,
the grass, a true lush green,
bold white cliffs, a perfect day.
Walking out on Beachy Head,
the two of us together,
a long climb out of the town,
up from the busy pier.

We read about another couple,
on Beachy Head that day,
with their dead son in a rucksack,
and his toys in another,
unutterable love in their hearts,
and the sky and the grass meant nothing.
And the cliffs were a means to an end.

Near death experience

Some information you can't process all at once,
arriving when you least expect it, which is at any time at all.
After lunch, the girl behind you is on the phone,
in front, in the middle of the room the manager stands
nervously. Everyone captured, one by one falling silent,
behind you the girl on the phone is still unaware.
The manager is speaking softly but you missed the crucial fact
". . . severe illness. No easy way to tell you . . . he's dead . . ."
The dead word echoes in your head blocking those that follow.
Behind you the girl signs off cheerily, suddenly becomes
perturbed.
You turn to the person next to you – "Who?",
spend the afternoon telling those who missed the news,
trying to believe a word you say, even as you say it.
In two's and three's people talk in corridors and corners.
When you can't trust yourself you walk the building,
taking a 'short cut' through the basement.
Work continues until it's time to leave,
Nobody has cried, nobody has hugged or even touched.
At times like this you remember all the other tragedies:
colleagues who died, whose children died
and those who survived and battled past the stroke,
the meningitis, the depression. At times like this
you hate yourself, drink whisky in the corner of the pub,
write bad poetry, go home alone. At times like this
you regret that you never got to know him.

Pivotal

I'm years away from the decision that it's time to go
but this is work not home and here I'm failing too.
I'm sitting in this room, staring at my hands
and I've absolutely no idea what I'm going to say.

I've got five minutes to collect my thoughts
but they're spinning madly, impossible to catch.
I shouldn't even be here, it was meant to all be fixed;
I was feeling better, stronger – all under control . . .

but it wasn't was it; just a false dawn, another self-defeating
house of cards, half buried by the sand.
I'm sitting in this room, staring at my hands
and I've absolutely no idea what I'm going to say.

I'm under so much pressure. I'm watched at every turn,
every tiny slip-up, every error, every time I even yawn,
"Not pulling his weight" . . . "Letting down the team."
Other people can relax but my cards have been marked.

Marked cards with ragged corners, impossible to stack
and the tide is coming in, washing them away.
I'm sitting in this room, staring at my hand
and I've absolutely no cards left to play.

She will want an answer, the time is nearly up
and I guess she has a right to one but I know that it's not fair
and anyway its not like I've got three magic words,
three words to turn my life around and give some kind of hope.

The door! Oh god I've nothing,
there is nothing I can say.
I'm sitting in this room, staring at my hands
and I've absolutely nothing left to say.

She walks in, I look up and say "I am depressed"
and it's like a weight is lifting from my chest.

The killer next-door

This man has a broken monster howling in his soul,
seeking love amidst the shards of devastated lust.
It understands the evil ones, stripped of all restraint,
conjuring the elemental devils in the dust.

Having no power they seek it.
Out of control they seize it.
Out of despair, they no longer care
what they lose to achieve it.

He's all alone: – I'm worried about the company he keeps:

"The water's running out and the sea is deep,
with blood. And the turning of the tide
heralds the coming of the flood.

It's not fair, it's not fair, it's <u>never</u> fair.
When I needed him, he wasn't there.
When I needed her, she spurned me."

Now only pain can set him free,
cut loose the fear that binds him.
He will eat his beating heart,
disassociate his soul,
and make the monster whole.

Absorbed by the emptiness within,
feeding the bonfire of his dark desire,
this thing that he's possessed by is all he does possess:

"Let it shine, let it shine,
make the holy terror MINE!!!"

Dysfunctional 2

It's so damn thin,   this forced harmony we're living in.
One more chink   and all the dark comes rushing in.
It's all spin,   the promises that took us in.
Don't try to think   there is no way that you can win.
Is this your skin   that's trying to keep your anger in?
One more drink   and all the walls come crashing in.
Sit still within   the broken shell but don't give in.

Anxiety – Sonnet #222

Tendrils of doubt prise the barriers apart.
This way; sit down; let the nightmares start.

All the truth that can't be faced
descends in echoes to the core,
locked behind the crumbling door:
The words with poison laced.
The words that whispered in through dreams,
that leak from unprotected seams.

Can you hear them calling?
       They are insidious and cruel.
Can you feel them crawling?
       Like moths in lighter fuel.

So we live, so we learn,
So we flutter and we burn.

Try to understand

She woke this morning calm and in control
ten minutes later she's in terror for her soul
clinging to the rim of the deepest darkest hole

She's no idea what's going on inside her head
descending to a nightmare pit of total dread:
here before her feet every nameless fear is spread.

. . . Fading now it leaves her tense.
She knows that she is mad. It makes no sense.
She can't prove this, she has no evidence.

Her dreams were soft they held no threats.
There were no night-terrors, no clammy sweats.
There's nothing to explain these feelings she gets.

Learning to swear   Learning to let go

Leaving the bathroom with the tap on,   water running, overflowing.
Anything bad could happen.   Anything bad will happen, has happened.
Already the firemen are coming.   The firemen will evacuate the building.
The building will be flooded.   The firemen will drown.
No knowing what could happen,   what will happen, has happened,
such reckless abandon,   such flagrant disregard,
there are rules about such things,   rules that keep us safe.
Repeat the rules, retrace each step.   The tap is running down the drain.
Next week we leave the building,   go outside to busy streets,
go outside to busy streets;   walk down crowded London roads.
And we shall be instructed to explete;   told to swear in public,
uttering profanities loudly;   talking rudely more than once.
You probably think this is amusing,   you may think that this is funny,
perhaps you should reread it,   it may help to make you understand.
Keep a count, add one to it   if the count is less than fifty read
the page

again.

Be brave

I suffer from mental health issues.
This makes me human: nothing more and nothing less.

My life became frozen by glacial progression,
leaving me in isolated wastes of still warm sorrow.
Lack of sleep ensured my survival, meant
that I remember little of those times.
And always I soldiered on: Kept my job
just: Held on to hope – just.

It could have been much worse . . .
But the problem is, it hasn't gone,
just receded into silent thoughts.
Occasionally they grow again – the doubts, the angst,
the nagging knowledge of my failings:
        past and future, real, imagined
but always crushing and complete
        nothing more and nothing less.

The state of not knowing

for Ken

It took me years to come to terms,
decades to forgive you for blaming her,
for leaving us that way,
on the path between hatred and despair.

You should never have left that note,
you were always much better than that.
But then I never read your words,
only heard second-hand reports.
Maybe you only tried to explain
how you came to feel so low.
So much your family kept from us –
even the method of your death.

Years later when I was looking for a flat,
the agent showed me yours, not knowing
he offered me the chance to live where you died;
to be where you bled, to breathe
where you suffocated, bathe where you
drowned, eat where you poisoned yourself,
to sleep with your ghost.

Between times

Under the roof, between the eaves,
we spent six months between lives,
looking forward and looking back,
listening to the distant thunder roll.
Two rooms containing bare essentials
and memories of everything we'd packed and sent away,
stored somewhere in the dark, separated by the rain,
from this limbo where we found ourselves,
making what-ifs by the beaded window,
watching the droplets merge
and run toward the sill.

The Quest for Knowledge

I feared memory too had died.
I struggled to remember;
then it came joyous and strong,
painful, as it should be –
nothing wrong.

Mythmatics – Sonnet #153

153 = 1³ + 5³ + 3³

The narcissistic number loves itself so much
the sum of each digit cubed adds up to itself.
You've got to love maths to feel the touch
of myths and legends within the wealth
of numbers. So you take this number,
break it down into the digits on the page,
like the youth who fell in slumber,
on the margin of a lake, in another age,
when a nymph was reduced to a dying refrain,
spurned by this youth, who loved no other face,
who took each feature magnified by itself, by itself again
and summed those parts back into place,
till he lost all sense of self, became a flower,
reflected in the ripples, hour after hour after hour.

The loss of innocence – Sonnet #14

That precious moment when the whole brain blinks;
suddenly the mass of blurred half-hidden forms
is lifted up, polished, painted and joined with interlocking links.
Standing still the whole world shudders, and transforms
about you, the new master of the universe.
It doesn't last of course: – After you step back
you see it's just a part that has grown obvious.
You spin it up and turn it round, acquire the knack
of knowing it from every viewpoint. It is yours.
You own it, all its beauty, all its grace;
every turn and corner and all its flaws,
how it can deform or be disgraced,
how it comes apart and how it breaks,
what it gives and what it takes.

Dream worlds – Sonnet #196a

That precious moment when the whole brain blinks;
from one state to the next, a sudden switch –
tripped. Things follow on but nothing links
and everything seems less real, more rich:
not dreams as wish fulfilment but dreams as life;
a third of all the time we have we spend
processing, connecting; we wield the subtle knife
that cuts away the hours and seconds that offend
our sense of value or our sense of pride,
that would not let us form our simple view
of who we are. The occurrences that we decide
are relevant and whether good or bad are labelled true.
In sleep we form the world afresh, within the limits of our brain.
By day we play, at night we shuffle through the deck again.

Science and faith – Sonnet #196b

Suddenly the mass of blurred half-hidden forms
came into focus beneath the Dutchman's eye
and stranger still the secrets that could live and die,
in every drop of water. Scientific storms
and tides redefined the world we knew;
it grew too much for one person to see.
Knowledge built on knowledge exponentially
and the many had to trust the rigour of the few.
It's so tempting for the ignorant to say it isn't so
while skimming over evidence, selectively, online;
pontificating socially over a glass of beer or wine,
confusing crackpot theories with things we really know.
There's far more knowledge than any can retain
and discrediting lies takes too long to explain.

She – Sonnet #196c

. . . is lifted up, polished, painted and joined with interlocking links
but isn't upgraded or given a heart and lung transplant,
worse there's no concern, for what it is that's renovated,
for how she breathes and loves or what she thinks.
There is no point in looking perfect if she can't
be happy in herself—rotten wood should never be gold plated.
Pygmalion didn't sculpt his lover out of crumbling stone
and if he had (would gods have laughed at him?)
most likely the spell would fail . . .
But then, Greek gods were shallow to the bone
and rarely bothered about what lay within,
happy, at a whim, to change a man entirely,
altering the form but leaving the soul unchanged,
to taste the pain of knowing it is but isn't him.

Lightning catcher – Sonnet #196d

Standing still the whole world shudders and transforms,
to leave you seeming far behind and lost.
You can't keep pace the way you used to do.
You once caught lightning, chasing storms,
never thinking of the hardship or the cost.
Now your electric days are through.
And the latest gadgets leave you cold,
fulfilling desires you're sure you never understood.
You don't need these things, any more than they need you.
The past is gone, the future's being sold
and nothing falls the way it should.
You don't know what you're holding onto
but you carry forward all the things you were or knew,
while everything you ever were is still as true.

The tyrant's lair – Sonnet #196e

About you the new master of the universe.
It's always about you and what you want from me.
You used to be a blessing, now my oath's a curse;
please, if you still love me, set me free!
God knows you have your cross to bear
or should, because you often tell Him so,
while blaming Him for never being there;
tell me, is that how it's supposed to go?
I know if I was in His place . . .
and in this respect I often am . . .
but I don't have His patience or His grace
and I'm past that point where I don't give a damn.
While, if I loved you more I might say less:
know this – I name you Ming the Merciless.

Losing control – Sonnet #196f

It doesn't last of course: – After you step back
that feeling you escaped this time,
for the others all took two steps back
and you're still standing in the firing line.
You know now that they set you up,
remember every entrance when the chatter stopped.
they pretended friendship, a loving cup –
inside a little poison dropped,
dissolving away your trust and belief
in the honesty of your fellow man;
Label him swindler, conman, thief –
see right through to his hidden plan.
The truth is an unwelcome guest –
it's you against the rest.

Ghosts and echoes in the air – Sonnet #196g

You see it's just a part that has grown obvious:
everything else still obscure behind the dust
unaware of changing fashions, oblivious
to the crumbling flakiness of paint and rust
that works upwards from the dampness
of the leaf-strewn hardwood floor.
Abandoned dereliction, shut away from progress,
locked away behind the peeling entrance door,
from dancing feet and floor-length gowns,
polished shoes synchronised to vanished tunes,
that seem somehow to linger in the run-down
memories of genteel afternoons.
What used to be the simple pleasures of a distant world
become sad feelings in which our autumn days lie curled.

Regaining control – Sonnet #196h

You spin it up and turn it round, acquire the knack
of playing God within the limits of your own internal
understanding.
You can take the clock and run it forward, turn it back,
take truth out for a spin, evaluate the handling
around the wicked bends – and on the straight
you press your foot down – hard to the floor
then slam on the brakes and wait
for the arrival of the law –
of motion – . . . – and then you skid.
That pause, between cause and effect,
that was something that you did.
You chose which rules you will ignore and which respect,
here inside, where the whole of reality is twirled –
around your little finger. This is your world.

Of – Sonnet #196i

Knowing it from every viewpoint. It is yours.
Feeling every facet, know you own it:
possessiveness (the hiding behind doors)
keeping trapped within everything that will fit
and much that claims the need to breathe,
that desires to see the light, feel the sun.
But you, too fearful it may choose to leave,
revealing a hole with all the ties undone
and you left powerless to make it right,
to capture it once more, force it back,
squeeze it in safe and jam it down tight.
Inside this want, this need, this maniac
impels control, makes ownership complete
and renders mere possession obsolete.

Beauty and grace – Sonnet #196j

You own it, all its beauty, all its grace,
although you can be sure it owns you too.
It knows your heart, it knows your face,
the superficial and the true.
It can twist your purpose, make you act
in ways you never thought you should.
It clouds your judgement, makes rumours fact,
makes right from wrong, turns won't to would.
But sometimes it can work its will to make
you better than you ever thought to be:
pulls out the lonely bitter seeds, to take
you gently by the hand, to climb above and see
the world again, renewed, refreshed with each heartbeat,
inside and out and all around complete.

When you were comatose – Sonnet #196k

Every turn and corner and all its flaws,
silent now. I used to love your cluttered rooms,
but now see bare, dry and dust-free floors,
a series of empty grieving tombs
where the air lies as still as death;
all those random sparks – gone out.
But, while there remains a gentle breath,
I'll wait and hope in fear and doubt.
If you would return and reignite
I'd greet each overflowing madcap thought
with unrestrained delight.
I loved the way your insight caught
on some detail, you always saw straight through,
overlooked by many, always so clear to you.

A world away – Sonnet #1961

How it can deform or be disgraced,
tested past all limits and yet endure,
weakened, diminished and defaced,
denied all respite or cure
and yet, buried deep inside,
denied nutrients it needs to thrive,
the only option left to hide
and yet, and yet it's still alive.
This is what we're searching for.
This is why we came so far,
to this barren desolation to explore
and seek out something on a par
with the simplest life we know
but alien and wholly new.

Find your own way back – Sonnet #196m

How it comes apart and how it breaks
is only ever partly understood;
what it is that causes it, what makes
everything we had, all that was good,
irrelevant, like water half a mile downstream,
just out of sight and never coming back.
Later, insubstantial, a fading dream,
lost in morning's glare. An emptiness, a lack,
as our former life sluggishly decays
but also independence, self reliance,
the chance to reassess how we spend our days,
whether we require love, mere dalliance
or solitude. A time alone to contemplate
our individuality, our ideal state.

Fundamental truths – Sonnet #196n

What it gives and what it takes
seems quite unfair. This poisoned apple,
the sharp discriminating fruit, that wakes
in us so much with which we need to grapple.
It gives us insights, strange and deep,
teaches, educates, expands the mind
but shakes us from contented sleep,
fearful of what it is that we will find
and how it can be used, abused.
Peeled back, our faith is the discarded rind
that reveals transgressions bruised
deep into the flesh. We retreat confused,
unable to assimilate the core, the concentrate:
fundamental secrets the hard pips store, inviolate.

The myth of predetermination – Sonnet #3

In every book there is a pattern, perfect and exact,
each page, line or word follows the one before
but that is true in fiction and this is true in fact:
belief in predetermination is a fatal flaw.
In this existence events only seem to happen
in a sequence. After each tragic episode
a new beginning will come in time and then
we think we see the journey back along the road;
without the myriad of might-have-beens;
the amorphous future is distilled into the past
and we pick and choose our way between the scenes,
until we come to see the truth, at last,
as fate. In every disaster we look for something good
but nothing really happens for a reason
                         – *we* add *that* afterwards.

A New Arrangement

We pass from day to day,
along constant well worn tracks,
held by the landscape of our lives
and the orbits of the stars,
until the earth shakes and the sky falls
and everything is new.

Just then

What happened then?
All the repercussions that began to flow
from one second's infinite events;
some of them may change my life
in ways I cannot guess;
some may fire a poem or realise a dream.

Subtraction – Sonnet #501

Subtracting myself from photographs
seamlessly, effortlessly, without any care:
I am very simply no longer there.
Nor ever was, no smiles, no laughs –
not mine – no involvement in any way.
I am freed from every aspect of my past;
no associations can hold me fast.
Only this body is mine today,
whatever went before has been released, repented.
That was a stranger, wearing my face,
just another member of the human race.
Someone quite unlike me your memory invented.
My past subtracted, reduced to nothing more
than dead leaves rustling outside the door.

After a period of absence – Sonnet #155

Escape into this world again;
a world renewed: with a sprightly wagtail,
darting over water, bobbing every step,
every beat of her tiny heart.

What was I thinking in those spirals?
What was I sinking ever further into?
I'm happy not to push the point
past what comes unbidden;

just retain enough to mark the path
and turn away towards the flash of yellow,
the slate grey back as soft as hope,
the darting beak and dipping tail:
tip to tail in every instant, whole, complete
and delicate as only life can be.

A game of chess – Sonnet #64

And shall I ever love again, or hold
myself in check and play such games no more?
Each night you kept your queen on ice, my bold
attacks repulsed. Your pawns revealed no door:
forlorn my probing failed to open any file.
I battered knights against your rooks as mine,
from lack of space, hung back the while,
in corners, spent and waiting to resign.

A reject does reject in turn his fate
and play where passive tactics hold less sway.
Lets make this clear you drove me from stalemate
to here and now I drive: My balls will play
on greener soil and swap the rough for smooth
fairway and hence my handicap improve.

Insight

Let failure come to my embrace,
not once or twice but every day.
Humdrum my verses lacked all grace
and failure came to my embrace,
with nothing falling into place,
till form and rhyme combined to say:
let failure come to my embrace,
not once or twice but every day.

My humdrum thoughts linger . . .
lifeless ink upon the page,
before a whispered breath

sparks latent embers,
giving rise
to fiery metamorphoses
birthing taloned phoenix birds:
bright eyes reflecting
each flaming
feathered form.
Each unexpected
wing-beat
heralding
the perfect storm.

Forgiveness – Sonnet #2

for Ken

Patting pockets, I feel the edge of keys
before closing the flat door behind me,
descending past my neighbours' doors.
My customary taking of the evening air,
leads me where paving stones run down
to the witness of calm lake waters
between the slanting branches and the dusk.
So we walked together yesterday,
you offering your good advice
for all my current concerns.
Today we smile, sharing passing observations,
remembering our better days, before I turn for home.
This is the way of it between old friends,
the present and the past.

Happy getting over me day

The legal papers arrived today, many years too late,
from the jaws of complacency, the slow defeat of fate;
a monument to failure, dropping like a stone,
the shame of broken memories in an abandoned home.
Sold up, sold out and moving on,
we can't put right what we made wrong.
There is not much more that we can say
but separately we share this day.

Self discovering

Knowledge begins with that of self,
self-referential, honest, open, true
not the selfish denial of others
but opening one's heart to the world:
pinned back with compassionate love,
sides pulled out to reveal the soft curled
cradle of the soul, suffuse with blood
pumping understanding to the toes, the fingertips,
the brain. Oh you have to love that brain,
fount of all your inspiration – all your subtle genius.

Only after turn it to your purpose
and it will cut through confusion
and pluck something extraordinary from
the hidden territories within and offer it
to the world outside – a song,
a theorem, a piece of engineering,
its form in harmony with the mind that birthed it
Your knowledge, Your discovery – *Your* Self.

Labels – Sonnet #1101

This condition that I might have,
I've had this set of symptoms all my life
                or might have.
I don't know if I want to know

if you think I have it too.
Who wants a label, especially one
that says your brain is different,
               not quite normal,

as if normal actually exists.
There are things you will never do
and others that you struggle with.
But that's always true, isn't it,

without the label or the stigma,
just like we all have things we're good at.

November memories

Kicking leaves in Embankment Gardens;
the years that fell, the hearts that hardened,
so separate now, in time and space,
the truth lies cold upon my face.
A keening seagull circles down
but all our hopes have long since flown.
We meet now, when we meet, as friends,
as tides that passed these river bends
and drifted out towards the distant sea,
where wind and rain and thoughts are free.

Imprints 1 – Sonnet #1051a

We share our fingerprints,
that young man in the photograph and I.
What does it mean that I remember
a few of the places where he left them?

So many surfaces forgotten, dusted,
swept, rubbed down and washed away.
I would dip my fingers in paint, apply them to the back
of a cave wall for future generations,

if I thought they were exceptional.
Delete my emails after I am gone,
take down my pages, dissolve my presence.
I would pass like a ghost from you,

light as a kiss from a loving father's lips – blown, flown,
with everything I ever touched and everything I own.

Imprints 2 – Sonnet #1051b

We share our fingerprints,
between the prison bars of taken choices.
What does it mean that I remember
that touch before we went our separate ways?

The cascade of minuscule decisions
cannot be undone, retraced, reset:
like piling water droplets up
to turn back time and resurrect a waterfall,

to capture the single misguided eddy,
that steered our barrel from a safer course,
causing it to splinter on the rocks below
and throw us out on lone trajectories,

to swim and cling to driftwood,
bound for different shores.

Imprints 3 – Sonnet #1051c

We share our fingerprints,
that younger self and I, you say.
What does it mean that I remember
or forget what that man did, or didn't do.

He made his choices in a different world –
misled, betrayed, perhaps . . .
or too damn weak to stand his ground,
amid a desperate maelstrom of destruction.

I can't give you the answers that you seek,
can't admit or refute your allegations
for I remember only hazy, shifting moments
from a lifetime you say I should regret.

In truth you've come too late; that man you seek,
whether I was he or not, that man is lost.

Imprints 4 – Sonnet #1051d

We share our fingerprints,
though that was June and this November.
What does it mean that I remember
the broken promises, the hints

of what we might have had together,
before the love and hate became too dense
and collapsed to numb indifference,
as we ran from stormy to inclement weather.

If I could meet that younger self,
could I tell him of the hollow loneliness,
the damage and the wastefulness
to physical and mental heath?

And this, this self-pity, this regret,
I need to let it go, resolve, forget.

Imprints 5 – Sonnet #1051e

Not just the fingerprints but the map of veins within your arm,
the pattern on your retina, the connections in your brain,
Each unique in every sense and detail,
so why do we all make the same mistakes?
Despite the variations we're more alike than different;
unable to break the bonds of evolution, history, culture
and yet, by increments, we drive these forward,
slowly, with false starts and misadventures
and surely no consensus on the final goal,
or even on the current path. Perhaps that's best –
All humanity striving for a single goal:
like hoards of lemmings driven off the cliff
by some crazed entertainer, film maker . . .
No! Let us celebrate diversity instead.

Revelations

Are you living? Is this life?
everything balanced on a knife
edge. Dancing on a narrow ledge,
buffeted by angel wings, of terror and delight.
Half blinded by the light
touch of honesty and true site
of all your triumphs and disasters, passing right
before your eyes; before this dawn,
this moment when you stand reborn
and behold the wonders of the world,
unfurled, of dreams no fool could contemplate
and yet – there is no future set,
unless it is written in regret
across the lines of the possible.

Pressing back into the hard rock wall,
stone between the shoulder blades,
you bend till the vision fades
in mist.
Resist –
and greet the new day,
dreaming, as the children play.
Life is always on the edge of things,
looking forward, flexing wings
of pure desire . . .
running lightly through the fire.

The next moon landing – Sonnet #27

for Sue Austin

Wheelchair user on the moon:
moon buggy bouncing, built in power king
watch her go! Quick look soon
she's gone over the horizon taking
no risks, wholly in control
careening over the surface like Artemis.
This has always been her goal,
to show the freedom of her harness,
to challenge how we see an astronaut.
A different form of locomotion –
that wonderment of a new exciting thought;
the expression of raw emotion.
See the future, feel the pride,
let her take you on that ride.

Time – Sonnet #59

Each slow second rests lightly on the one before
but what a crushing weight our first ones bear.
Each tick ticks louder on the inner ear
until they build to endless toneless roar.
Each minute climbs towards the midnight hour.
From clock to calendar surging pressures weigh,
the momentum subtle-rises day on day.
The lengthening shadow of our mortal flower
plays out upon the spinning ground, the rock
that slides on continental drift. – But halt. –
Each point, each now I spend with you, is all,
in turn I fix it to the page, love-locked.
It cares not what is gone or what will pass,
each gentle second flattens down the last.

Carpe diem – Sonnet #111

Days of chaos theory, climate change,
inching ever closer to the tipping point,
between the familiar and the strange,
nothing smooth, all disjoint,
precarious and under attack
and oh so completely vulnerable.
There is no easy journey back
to the safety of the comfortable,
if lonely life, amidst suburban streets.
We take the switchback roller-coaster ride,
without the safety bar, without the seats!
Nowhere to conceal the excitement inside,
we take our chances, seize the day.
I wouldn't have it any other way.

Seasoned

Oil, cold pressed from the crinkled kernel of the nut,
infusing sweet basil and green hearted lemon thyme,
as clear and subtle as last summer's sun,
that soaked into each herby leaf in turn,
slowly settling out in bottled days of morning mists
and each autumnal evening's cool dipped shadow tips.

Leaving

So when a man's about to die or near the end of days he pays for men to dig a well, that others may have water free to drink, that's cool and pure and clear.

Or plants a tree he carefully selects, to spread the gift of shade to guests, who will, in times to come, pass through on their own paths to God (may peace be found with Him).

And so he leaves a gift of perfect hospitality, that lives beyond his life and honours those, perhaps unborn, that he will never meet.

Coda

The poetry of gravity,
where short utterances speak of loss
and hold us locked in shared experiences,
orbiting each other, poet and listener,
connected by the sound-wave field,
where words bend the fabric of our lives.

The poetry of entropy,
where line by line
the writing gives way
to the blank white void,
where sounds
               splash
                       into
                               stillness.

And now

This present time is such a gift.
There will never be another time like this,
balanced between whatever will be fated
and whatever it was that has already been
lies this single moment, forever recreated;
in it alone the very stuff of life is seen.

Nick Alldridge - Biography

Nick Alldridge lives in South London where he is a regular at Poets Anonymous and Beyond Words. He is co-editor of Poetic Licence Magazine (www.poeticlicencemagazine.com) which publishes poetry and flash fiction. His poems have previously been published in South Bank Poetry, Poetic Licence (under previous editors), First Time and in translation in Poezja dzisiaj in Polish. He recently had a poem in 154 an anthology of poems by 154 contemporary poets in reply to Shakespeare's sonnets published by Live Canon.

Palewell Press

Palewell Press is a small independent publisher handling poetry, fiction and non-fiction with a particular interest in human rights, social history, and the environment. Writers on these subjects who are looking for publication should, in the first instance, send ten pages of their work to enquiries@palewellpress.co.uk

Lightning Source UK Ltd.
Milton Keynes UK
UKOW01f0852210916

283478UK00002B/43/P